—— joy redefined ——

LOVING JESUS

Printed in the United States of America.

First Printing, 2018

ISBN 978-1-942854-61-6

Joyce Meyer Ministries
P.O. Box 655
Fenton, Missouri 63026
joycemeyer.org

MEET THE
LOVE OF YOUR LIFE

Have you dreamed of meeting the love of your life? You can. His name is Jesus.

God wants to be part of your life in the most intimate way. He wants to be part of your coming and your going. He knows you better than anyone else, but do you know Him? Are you making decisions in your life based on rules or based on your relationship with Him?

One of the most important things I believe God has called me to do is to help people experience the joy of the Lord through new life as believers in Christ (see 2 Corinthians 5:17), and the deep satisfaction of a life lived boldly for Him, serving others.

Through the example of His Son and your relationship with Him, you can learn to enjoy your life *now*, this very moment. If you will turn your heart to Jesus and devote yourself completely to knowing Him, your life can be **blameless and guileless, innocent and uncontaminated...without blemish in the midst of a [morally] crooked and [spiritually] perverted generation, among whom you are seen as bright lights [beacons shining out clearly] in the world [of darkness]** (Philippians 2:15).

Pleasing God is not about rules, and it's not about following a religion. Being a Christian is about relationship—a personal relationship with Jesus. Too many people believe the way to please God and get to that shining place of joy is by following "the rules." If you'll do this or give up doing that, God will be pleased with you. Then you'll be blessed. Then you'll experience joy.

There are lots of us who love rules. Rules make us feel safe. We say, "Just tell me what to do, and I can do it." Except we can't— that's why we need Jesus. On our own, we can never earn or do enough good to deserve the unconditional love and forgiveness that's offered to us through the sacrifice Jesus made for us. His love, mercy and grace are given as gifts; we just have to receive them.

The truth is, Jesus did not die so we can have a religion based on works. He died so we can have a relationship born of love.

God wants you to know the difference between religion and having a personal relationship with Him. God wants you to understand how unfruitful and dissatisfying religion can be, and He wants you to know how relationship sets you free. Jesus is the Way to God (see John 14:6), and relationship with Him is the path to begin enjoying life and enjoying God.

So I want to help you concentrate on your relationship with Jesus. Remember what Paul said, ***I want to know Christ . . . to know the power of his resurrection . . .*** (Philippians 3:10 NIV). If you make knowing Jesus the most important thing in your life . . . if He's the love of your life, then everything else will fall into place.

WE NEED TO
GET TO THE
POINT WHERE
WE DO GOOD
THINGS BECAUSE
WE LOVE GOD . . .

NOT TO TRY
TO GET HIM
TO LOVE US.

CHAPTER ONE

The amazing thing about Jesus is that He includes everybody in His circle of love, and He excludes nobody.

When Jesus walked on earth, He had the most trouble with the religious folks, especially a sect called Pharisees, known for their self-righteous attitudes. Religious people are usually critical and judgmental. And if you're not like *them,* then you're not part of their group.

I was a religious person for a long time. I would have made a great Pharisee if I had lived in Jesus' day. I was one of those people who continually strived to keep the rules so I could feel good about myself. I couldn't believe that God could love me just as I was, right where I was in my life. Maybe you can relate to what I'm talking about.

Religion is filled with rules and regulations—all the things that *religious* people think they have to do to be acceptable to God. One woman put it really well. She heard me speaking in a meeting about not being religious, and when she didn't really understand what I meant, she prayed and asked God what I meant. He said, "Religion is man's idea of My expectations." I think that's interesting and right on target.

IT'S NOT ABOUT BEING GOOD

What do you think God expects from you? You might think, *Well, He expects me to be good.* No, He doesn't. He already knew, before you were born, you weren't going to be good. The only goodness you have is His goodness shining through you. We need to receive the sacrifice Jesus made for us when He died on the cross, so we can become right with God (see 2 Corinthians 5:21).

We need to get to the point where we do good things *because we love God*...not to try to get Him to love us. A good thing is not really any good unless it's done for the right reason.

There are a lot of people in the world who can do *good things.* The world may think they're good, but God doesn't think they're good because their motive is not right. They're doing *good things* to be seen. They're doing *good things* to be noticed. They're doing *good things* for people to like them. They're doing *good things* so they can feel good about themselves.

Some people get all their worth and value out of being caretakers. They spend their lives trying to find somebody who they can take care of. But they're not doing it because they love the other person; they're doing it because it makes them feel good about themselves.

God wants us to do what we do because **we love Him,** out of obedience to Him, and with pure motives just to help somebody else—not to impress Him or have an attitude that says, "Now God owes me. I've earned His blessing."

For example, if you pray four hours a day, that doesn't mean you're entitled to a problem-free life. When you do have a problem, if you hear yourself saying, "I don't understand how this could happen to me. Why did this happen to me? I pray four hours every day! I go to church every week. I'm faithful. I tithe. I teach Sunday school. I don't understand, God, how this could happen to me!" just remember, we're not serving God so we never have a problem or a struggle in life. We're serving God because He's awesome, because we love Him, and He's worthy of our best!

Religious people don't enjoy God. They don't enjoy life. Everything is about the rules and the regulations. I really want you to get this: You can make a "law"—something you think you have to do to be good enough—out of anything. You can make a law out of exercise, or cleaning house, or prayer. You can even make a law out of Bible reading.

WHAT THE DEVIL
WANTS FOR YOUR LIFE

I want to make sure you understand what I mean by "law." It's a rule that you set for yourself because you believe it's required for you to be acceptable or okay. Now, I'm not saying discipline is not good, and there's nothing wrong with having guidelines to follow. You can even have some rules that you live by if you want to. But if the laws you set for yourself become legalistic, then you'll feel guilty and condemned every time you don't do them. *I didn't read the Bible today. I can't expect God to bless me now! I fell asleep when I was praying. I forgot to give an offering at church last week. I bet God is mad at me.* I'm pretty confident I'm not the only one who has had these thoughts!

The devil wants to put a burden on us

so we always feel bad about something, and no matter what we're doing, it's not enough or it's never good enough. He will try to condemn you with thoughts such as, *It doesn't really matter if I read my Bible, because I won't remember anything I read.*

It's also easy to get discouraged about prayer. Have you ever felt that even when you do pray, you aren't doing it "right" and it doesn't seem that God heard your prayers?

But when our focus is having a relationship with God, we see these activities as fellowship with Him...time spent in His presence, discovering who He is and who we are meant to be.

I was talking with one of our employees about this and she shared a great perspective. She said, "I just wish that people knew how to make Christianity a normal part of their everyday life." And a friend of mine from Australia who ministers all over the world says, "We need to stop *acting* like a Christian and *be* one."

A lot of people seem to think that going to church is all they need to do to be a Christian. Many times when I've asked someone, "Are you a Christian?" they've told me what church they go to. But being a Christian is not just about going to church. Just as sitting in your garage all day won't make you a car, simply sitting in a church does not make you a Christian.

We need to understand how to become like Jesus in our thinking and our behavior. Because if you go to church but you're not allowing God to change your heart and make you more like Him, then you're going to be frustrated, discouraged, unhappy or unfulfilled. You're going to miss out on what God has for you through a relationship with Him.

The bottom line is this: No matter what you're doing, if you're doing it to impress God, or to impress yourself or other people … if you don't have any real relationship with God, then there's no fellowship.

Real Christianity is all about making your life in Christ an integral part of everything you do and being transformed into His image a little more every day. Understanding this and being committed to this lifestyle is the key to experiencing true joy!

For it is by grace you have been saved, through faith—and this is not from yourselves, it is the gift of God—not by works, so that no one can boast.

—Ephesians 2:8-9 NIV

And you, who once were alienated and enemies in your mind by wicked works, yet now He has reconciled in the body of His flesh through death, to present you holy, and blameless, and above reproach in His sight—if indeed you continue in the faith, grounded and steadfast, and are not moved away from the hope of the gospel which you heard....

—Colossians 1:21-23 NKJV

IT WAS LIFE-
CHANGING WHEN
GOD GAVE ME THE
REVELATION THAT
WHAT REALLY
MATTERS IS . . .

FOR ME TO KNOW
HIM AND TO SERVE
HIM BECAUSE
I LOVE HIM.

CHAPTER TWO

Many people have the life of God in them, but they do not really enjoy God or life.

Maybe you've experienced true relationship with God through Christ by simply receiving His gifts of love, grace and forgiveness of your sin. But there are so many people who are just fed up with religious rules and regulations. They are desperate to know Jesus and the power of His resurrection. They long to be free and know what it's like to be led by the Holy Spirit, not by a man-made list of do's and don'ts. They are tired of trying to fit into somebody else's box of what it means to be a Christian and know God.

Many times when somebody is born-again,

the first things they're told is how they should dress or what changes they need to make in their behavior. They hear things like: "Your hair is the wrong color. You shouldn't have that tattoo or body piercing. You're not wearing the right clothes," and the list goes on and on. Their introduction to Christianity is a bunch of rules. "You're going to have to cut that hair… You're going to have to do this."

This approach totally misses the heart of what it means to be a new creation in Christ (see 2 Corinthians 5:17). The most important change we can ever experience is a change of our heart. We need God to work in our soul—our mind, will and emotions—because that's the way we become Christians. But sadly, oftentimes churches get caught up in external things and preach at people to do certain things to be part of their religious organization.

Jesus didn't die so we could have a religion; He died so we could have a deep, passionate, personal relationship with God, so we could talk to God and hear Him speaking to our heart. So we could **approach God's throne of grace with confidence, so that we may receive mercy and find grace to help us in our time of need** (Hebrews 4:16 NIV).

Here's another amazing truth: God called Abraham His friend, and He wants you to be His friend!

James 2:23 says, . . . **"Abraham believed God, and this [faith] was credited to Him [by God] as righteousness and as conformity to His will," and he was called the friend of God.**

LEARNING TO BE
COMFORTABLE WITH GOD

When I teach about having fellowship with Jesus, I'm talking about having relationship with God, spending time with Him. The main meaning of the word *fellowship* is "communication." And communicating with God does not require eloquent language or speaking in a different tone.

My greatest desire is for you to get comfortable with God. This doesn't mean you are irreverent or disrespectful. It simply means you don't have to be afraid of Him. God doesn't want you to be afraid of Him.

There are a couple of ladies who have worked for me for many years and they often have lunch together. I'll find them sitting together in the kitchen area, both reading a section of the newspaper. Every once in a while, they'll put down the paper and make a comment—like an old married couple. After years of knowing each other, they know what the other is thinking or how she will react to the latest headline. That's how well God wants us to know Him—so well that even when He doesn't speak, we know what His heart is about the matter.

I believe the high call on every believer's life is to enjoy God.

John 10:10 is one of my favorite verses. It says: **The thief comes only in order to steal and kill and destroy. I came that they may have and enjoy life, and have it in abundance [to the full, till it overflows]**. It's very clear in this scripture that Jesus came so we can enjoy our lives, and have abundant life in Him!

But how can we enjoy life if we don't enjoy God? He is life. All life comes from Him. Sadly, many people are more focused on religion than relationship. And when it comes to serving God, they get all worked up about finding out what their gifts are, how they're supposed to be utilizing their gifts, and what His plan is for their life. They end up working at their ministry so much that they miss out on experiencing the presence of God and the joy that comes only in His presence.

After I was in ministry for about five years, I thought, *Ministry, ministry, ministry—life's got to be about more than going to meetings!*

Before I reached this point, I was just so

proud of myself because I worked for God. I remember thinking things like, *I'm in the ministry. And I go to early morning prayer three times a week. And I do this, and I do that, and I do something else.* But it wasn't really fulfilling or enjoyable because I was doing those things for the wrong reason.

It was life-changing when God gave me the revelation that what really matters is for me to *know Him* and to serve Him because I love Him. Doing "ministry" with a wrong motive—because it made me feel good about myself—wasn't bringing real joy to my life.

Matthew 7:22-23 talks about this. It says, ***Many will say to Me on that day [when I judge them], 'Lord, Lord, have we not prophesied in Your name, and driven out demons in Your name, and done many*** *miracles in Your name?' And then I will declare to them publicly, 'I never knew you; depart from Me . . . you who act wickedly [disregarding My commands].'*

Jesus wants us to know Him, and He wants us to have fellowship with Him. He wants us to communicate with Him—and He wants to communicate with us.

―――――――――――――――――――――

GOD WANTS US TO
COME INTO HIS
PRESENCE . . .

AND FELLOWSHIP
WITH HIM NOW,
IN THIS LIFE.

WE NEED GOD EVERY HOUR

I recall an old hymn titled, "I Need Thee Every Hour." If only we realized how true this is! God doesn't want to be your last resort that you use only when you have an emergency. Whether we know it or not, we are in desperate need of God all the time. And it's a mistake if we just pray when we feel out of control or that we have more in our hands than we can handle. Because the truth is, without His help, we won't do anything very well for very long.

Apart from Jesus, we can't accomplish anything that really matters from an eternal perspective.

If God's grace wasn't in our lives…if He wasn't helping us and protecting us, I don't know where we would be.

Think for a moment about Ephesians 3:12 (NIV), which says, ***In him and through faith in him we may approach God with freedom and confidence.*** This is what Jesus died for —forgiveness of our sins so we can approach God with freedom and confidence.

Our sins need to be forgiven so we can have fellowship with God. Because God is holy and completely righteous, we can't come into His presence as sinful human beings. It's just not possible because God cannot abide in the presence of sin. And more than anything else, He wants to fellowship with us and desires our companionship.

God loves us so much that He sent His only Son to die a horrible death and shed His blood so our sins could be washed away, and we could be completely cleansed—not just so we can go to heaven someday. While heaven is our ultimate destiny, God wants us to come into His presence and fellowship with Him now, in this life.

We don't have to shrink from God in fear. Instead, in humility, we can come boldly before Him, boldly to His throne of grace, and fellowship with Him. He wants us to come to Him to have our needs met, live powerful lives and be a witness to others of His amazing love and grace. And someday, yes, we can go to heaven and live a better life than we could ever have imagined.

What I want you to fully comprehend is that Jesus also wants us to enjoy Him while we're right here, right now. We won't be able to do that if we get up every day and think, *Oh, I have to pray. I have to read my Bible before*

I do anything else. You don't *have to do anything.* Prayer is a privilege; you *get* to talk to God. You *get* to pray and invite the power of God into your life for that day. You *get* to read God's Word, your instruction book for life that will keep you from having to repeat the same mistakes over and over, without the hope of ever being able to change.

The Bible contains answers for everything in life! Who wouldn't want to read it, study it, and know it? Who wouldn't want to read so much of it that it's rooted in your heart and mind, and becomes who you are? Who wouldn't want to walk in wisdom and have the knowledge and the gifts of God flowing through their life?

When we meditate on God's Word and it gets in our heart, the Holy Spirit can remind us of the scriptures we need, so we immediately know what we need to do in every situation.

OUR RELATIONSHIP GIVES US BOLDNESS

I love the Amplified version of Ephesians 3:12. It says, **In whom we have boldness and confident access through faith in Him [that is, our faith gives us sufficient courage to freely and openly approach God through Christ].**

Take a moment to really think about that. Because of the blood of Christ, we have been cleansed of our sins, and God views us as righteous. Second Corinthians 5:21 (NIV) says, **God made him who had no sin** *to be sin for us, so that in him we might become the righteousness of God.*

God doesn't want you wearing the filthy rags of guilt and condemnation, going around with your head hanging down, barely able to make it through life, feeling like God's mad at you all the time because of all the mistakes you make. Instead, He wants you to get your mind off yourself and get your mind on Him.

Those sins that you're fighting with—you will continue to fight with them until you get your mind off of them and start drawing near to Jesus, fellowshipping with Him. Because when you fellowship with Him, that's when you find the strength to overcome your sins.

The devil wants us to think, *Well, I better get myself straightened out so God's not mad at me … so I can have a relationship with Him.*

None of us can make ourselves acceptable to God without Christ.

James 4:8 (NIV) says, **Come near to God and he will come near to you. Wash your hands, you sinners, and purify your hearts, you double-minded.** Have you ever noticed that we're told to draw near to God <u>before</u> we're told to stop sinning? That one little detail could make a huge difference in so many people's lives.

Do you have any idea how many people there are in the world who think they can never come to God, can never have a relationship with Him, can never be a Christian, because they have issues in their lives that *they* are trying to overcome in their own strength? They're trying to get themselves all straightened out so they can be good enough to have a relationship with

God—and it just won't work.

*Jesus makes all the difference
in our life because without Him,
we can never be good enough.*

Scripture tells us that our righteousness —any good works that we can do on our own—is like filthy rags compared to the righteousness of God (see Isaiah 64:6). But Jesus' death on the cross and His shed blood paid the debt for our sins. That's why if we want to have a relationship with God, we go to Him in the name of Jesus. Because in Him, we have forgiveness.

In Jesus' name I can come boldly to God. I can come with an unreserved approach as often as I want and ask God for anything, because He never gets tired of me.

IF WE'RE ABIDING
IN JESUS, RATHER
THAN FOLLOWING
RELIGIOUS
RULES AND
REGULATIONS . . .

THEN WE WON'T
EVEN HAVE TO
STRUGGLE TO
BEAR FRUIT.

CHAPTER THREE

*Far too many of God's children
never enjoy their lives, because
they choose to walk their own way.*

I remember a woman from years ago who
lived in my daughter's subdivision. She went
to church every week. She had Christian
bumper stickers and all the signs announcing,
"I'm a Christian! I'm a Christian! I'm a
Christian!" But when we're *being* Christian,
we don't have to announce to everyone that
we are one.

For example, an apple tree doesn't stand
out in the middle of the field and yell, "I'm
an apple tree! I'm an apple tree! I'm an apple
tree!" It just produces apples, and everybody
knows what it is by the fruit that's on it.

If we're fellowshipping with God, abiding in Him as a vine is connected to the branches then we'll bear the right fruit. John 15:5 (NIV) says, *I am the vine; you are the branches. If you remain in me and I in you, you will bear much fruit; apart from me you can do nothing.* If we're abiding in Jesus, rather than following religious rules and regulations, then we won't even have to struggle to bear fruit.

RULES CRUSH THE SPIRIT OF GOD AND CUT THE LINES OF COMMUNICATION

Trying to keep certain rules and behave in ways that we think make us righteous doesn't get us anywhere. I used to get up in the morning and think, *I'm going to try to be good today. I'm going to try to be a good wife, and I'm going to try to keep my mouth shut, and I'm going to try to not get angry, and I'm going to try to be patient. God, I'm just so tired of trying. I try and I try, and no matter how hard I try, God, I always make mistakes! And I know You're just so fed up with me and I'm such a mess.*

Maybe you've thought, *Oh, God, if You'll just forgive me, God, just one more time, I promise I'll never do it again.* Oh yes, you will. Even if you don't make that particular mistake again, you'll do something else.

There's a difference between relationship and religion. Relationship is focused on God's love and grace—His power, given to us as a gift, to enable us to do with ease what we could never do with any amount of struggle or effort on our own. It's having a heart that desires to do what's right because we love God, not because we want to impress anyone or try to earn something from God.

Religion is all about "works of the flesh," and puts a burden on us, unlike God's grace. "Works" are accomplished through our own energy and are about us trying to do what only God can do in us and through us. We're doing works when we're following religious rules or regulations out of a sense of obligation to keep God happy with us or make ourselves acceptable to Him.

This approach steals the joy out of everything—prayer, Bible study, doing good deeds to help others, going to church—even our daily routine of life. It makes us feel like we have to do certain things to earn

God's love or favor, and leads to guilt and condemnation when we don't do everything we feel like we're supposed to do. It also makes us judgmental and critical of others because we aren't just trying to "keep the rules," but we're comparing how we measure up to others.

I think it's interesting, and sad, that God gave Moses the Ten Commandments and by the time Jesus came, the people had added 2,000 laws or rules they were supposed to live by that God didn't give! They were rules that were supposed to "help" people keep the original ten God gave them, but they ended up causing them to have religious attitudes and mindsets that kept them from real relationship with God.

FINDING FREEDOM

I am committed to teaching people how to be free in Christ. John 8:36 says, *If the Son makes you free, then you are unquestionably free.* That doesn't mean we are free to sin or to live sloppy lives, but it does mean we're free to follow the leadership of the Holy Spirit.

Following the Holy Spirit is a very practical part of living the Christian life, and it simply means we're obedient to Him. As born-again believers in Christ, the Holy Spirit lives in each of us. Ephesians 3:16 says God strengthens and energizes you *with power through His Spirit in your inner self, [indwelling your innermost being and personality].*

He comes to live in our hearts when we're born-again, and then He teaches and guides us according to God's plan and purpose for us. One way He does this is by convicting us of the sin in our lives, and we learn what's right and wrong as we grow in faith. As we spend time with Him every day, praying and studying the Bible, we develop sensitivity to His voice in our hearts, and we obey Him more and more.

Romans 8:14 (NIV) says, ***For those who are led by the Spirit of God are the children of God.*** In Christ, we can be led by the Holy Spirit because He lives in us. And we are free to obey Him because we love Him, and we know that everything He tells us to do, or not to do, is for our good. We just need to learn to follow His lead, confident that whatever He puts in our heart to do, He will give us the ability to do it!

Being obedient to God is not always easy, but it will always bring peace and joy as a result. When the Holy Spirit prompts you to do something, He gives you the grace to do it. But when somebody else tells you to do it, it's a burden because you feel like you have to do it to please them. It's so much better to obey God out of a heart that wants to be obedient because of love, not a sense of obligation to keep Him happy.

In 2 Corinthians 3:6, Paul says, ***He has qualified us [making us sufficient] as ministers of a new covenant [of salvation through Christ], not of the letter [of a written code] but of the Spirit; for the letter [of the Law] kills [by revealing sin and demanding obedience, but the Spirit gives life.*** Paul is saying here that as "ministers of a new covenant," our purpose is not just to go around and teach people rules and regulations they must follow. He has called us to teach people how to be led by the Holy Spirit. And because the Holy Spirit is the "Holy Spirit," He will work holiness through you. You'll end up living the life that God wants you to live, but you'll give Him the credit for it because you're not doing it through struggle, effort, rules, and regulations—you're doing it out of a relationship of love.

Remind yourself daily,
"I'm called to fellowship with God."

In 1 Corinthians 1:9 (NIV), Paul says, **God is faithful, who has called you into fellowship with his Son, Jesus Christ our Lord.** This is talking about communication, communion, sharing in common, making a contribution, having a partnership, being a partaker, and having a companion. But it really is like hanging out with a great friend or having the kind of relationship you're supposed to have in your marriage.

Fellowship with God is not just a one-hour church service on Sunday morning each week, throwing a little something in the offering plate to feel like you've done your part. Fellowship is an ongoing relationship, talking to God about everything—from the smaller details of your daily life to the major decisions you need to make. Should I marry this person? Should I buy this car? Is my attitude bad? Do I need to apologize? It's about everything.

Fellowship with God means you include Him in everything—in every part of your life.

DON'T MAKE
A PLAN AND THEN
PRAY FOR GOD
TO MAKE YOUR
PLAN WORK.

PRAY FIRST,
AND GET
GOD'S PLAN!

He's jealous of the other things in our lives that crowd Him out. Our God is a jealous God. He wants to be first in everything you do. He wants to be the first person you talk to in the morning. And when you have a problem, He wants to be the first person you talk to about it.

Don't run to the phone; run to the throne.

Hebrews 4:16 (NIV) says, **Approach God's throne of grace with confidence, so that we may receive mercy and find grace to help us in our time of need.** Don't call up one of your friends who doesn't even know what she's doing. Go to God. He may lead you to someone or He may lead someone to you. But it insults Him when we run to people and leave Him out.

I love Proverbs 3:6, which says, ***In all your ways know and acknowledge and recognize Him, and He will make your paths straight and smooth [removing obstacles that block your way].*** Acknowledging God just means we care about what He thinks about what we're doing. Don't make a plan and then pray for God to make your plan work. Pray first, and get God's plan!

Don't put the cart before the horse. We use that phrase all the time, but I thought through that scenario the other day, and it brought Dave to mind. He's wanted me to go on a carriage ride for about three years. I've been putting it off because I want everything to be just right—I want the right horse, the right day, the right city, and the right weather. I've been telling him things like, "Oh, it's too cold." "It's too hot." "That's an ugly horse." It made me think about what would happen if Dave and I actually did take a carriage ride and the cart was before the horse? What if we got in the cart and the horses were trying to either push the cart or walk backward to pull the cart. Of course, the cart would be going all over the place; there would be all kinds of problems steering it.

That's the way a lot of us are; we've just got things in our lives backwards. We're trying to be good so God will accept us, when He's throwing a come-as-you-are party. Through His Son, He's sent an invitation, saying, "Come to Me the way you are, and I'll help you be what you need to be."

God is the only one who can change you from the inside out. If you let Him, He will work those bad habits and bad behavior out of you, and He'll do it a little bit at a time, taking you from glory to glory (see 2 Corinthians 3:18). But the great thing about God is that when He tells you to change something, He gives you the strength, the grace, and the ability to do it. When people tell you to change something, they're not the ones who are going to help you make those changes.

———————————————

WITH GOD'S ANOINTING, YOU CAN ACCOMPLISH ANYTHING

Let's go back for a minute to the lady who lived in my daughter's subdivision and was so religious. She went to church every single Sunday without fail. Well, I was having a conference in town, and my daughter asked permission to put flyers up in the neighborhood about the conference. She put them on the mailboxes, which was not uncommon. This "religious" lady became so irate that she wanted to sue the subdivision because they put up *Joyce Meyer Ministries* flyers. She didn't like me because I'm a woman, and she didn't think I should be preaching.

That's the way religion is—you're not doing it the way I'm doing it, so there's something wrong with you. Oftentimes the first questions religious people ask are, "What are your credentials and what seminary did you go to? Do you know Greek and Hebrew?"

I don't know any of that. I didn't go to seminary. I don't have impressive academic titles. I'm just Joyce. I know God, and I'm continually learning more about Him. I know we have an enemy, the devil, and I know what he's like. I know what it's like to be hurt and wounded. I know what it's like to be healed. I know the Word and am a lifetime learner, studying it as much as I can every day. I know the Holy Spirit. I know Jesus.

I don't know a lot of the things "religious" people think are important, but God helps me to know what I need to know. I'm not belittling education. I'm not against having degrees. I think that's wonderful if that's the path God leads you to take. I'm simply making the point that while I didn't get that opportunity, it doesn't disqualify me from being used by God.

Speaking about Jesus, Isaiah prophesied, ***The Spirit of the Sovereign LORD is on me*** **[Jesus]*, because the LORD has anointed me to proclaim good news to the poor...*** (Isaiah 61:1 NIV). Jesus was anointed by the Holy Spirit to do His ministry on the earth, and as believers in Him, we have that same anointing. That means that in Christ, we can do whatever we need to do as long as we're in God's will, following His plan for our lives!

You can do anything God anoints you to do, and you don't have to fit into somebody else's "box," doing things the way they think you should do them. The best thing you can ever do is follow the wisdom of God, not the world. In 1 Corinthians 1:20 (NIV) the apostle Paul says, ***Where is the wise person? Where is the teacher of the law? Where is the philosopher of this age? Has not God made foolish the wisdom of the world?*** He's basically saying that God saved the world through the Gospel, which is considered foolish by those who do not believe it.

I don't have all the degrees, and I haven't mastered knowledge of Greek and Hebrew, but you know what I do have? God has given me a gift to teach His Word and a passion to help people discover the love, healing, transformation and freedom we can only find through Christ.

In addition to my gift of communication, I believe that one of the greatest gifts God has given me is common sense. Common sense can sometimes take you further in this life than education alone.

For example, if you want people to work for you and do excellent work, you've got to appreciate them. I didn't need to go to school to figure that out. That's just common sense. If you want to have good relationships, then you can't just demand to have your own way all the time. There's got to be a give and take on both sides. That's also common sense. If you don't want to be in debt, don't buy more than you can pay for. And here's another good one: If you don't want to be overweight, don't eat more calories than you're going to burn. And if you want a clean house, clean it. It's as simple as that.

God loves you so much, and He wants you to enjoy your relationship with Him and enjoy your life as you walk out His plans and purposes for you. You are ***God's handiwork, created in Christ Jesus to do good works, which God prepared in advance for us to do*** (Ephesians 2:10 NIV).

As you love Him and serve Him because you love Him, you'll experience more joy in the life He's called you to live!

YOU CAN BE
AS CLOSE TO GOD
AS YOU WANT
TO BE; IT ALL
DEPENDS ON . . .

HOW MUCH
TIME YOU'RE
WILLING TO
PUT INTO YOUR
RELATIONSHIP
WITH HIM.

CHAPTER FOUR

We have to do what we do because we love God, not to impress Him or to earn something from Him.

———————————

As I said before, the difference between religion and relationship has to do with the motives of your heart. Why are you doing what you're doing for God? Do you find yourself falling into a religious attitude, motivated to do good works because it makes you feel good about yourself? Most people have a struggle with this at some time in their lives. Pride is a very dangerous attitude to have!

In Luke 18:9-14, Jesus tells a parable about two men, a Pharisee and a tax collector, who went to the temple to pray. The Pharisee was a religious leader who followed the rules, fasted twice a week and gave exactly what was required of his finances. And he was proud of it! See, when you follow the rules, you want others to know about it. You want to be admired.

Verse 9 says Jesus was talking **to some who were confident of their own righteousness and looked down on everyone else** (NIV). Religious people trust in themselves and are confident that they are righteous; they scorn and look down on everyone else. But the tax collector was a different story. He humbly prayed to God, confessing his sin, sincerely pleading for mercy. Jesus said he was justified before God because his heart motive was right.

If we're not doing what we do for the right

reasons, our heart is not right with God. We should do what we do *because we love God,* not to impress Him or to earn His love and approval. Matthew 6 is a great chapter of Scripture that teaches us what our motives should be. The bottom line is, if we're doing good works to impress people and be admired by them, we will have no reward from our Father in heaven.

DOING WHAT'S RIGHT FOR THE RIGHT REASON

I want to say it again: God wants us to do what we do because we love Him. He wants us to pray each day because we love Him and because we know that He's the only one who can help us. Without Him we're nothing, and apart from Him we can do nothing (see John 15:5). He wants us to read and study the Word because there is life in His Word. We know that Jesus is the Word made flesh (see John 1:1), and when we study Scripture, we discover the heart of God.

There's inherent power in the Word to strengthen us to do what we should do (see Hebrews 4:12), when we do it for the right reasons. It pleases God, and we experience His joy. But when we do things for wrong reasons, it can make us mean, critical, judgmental, and cause us to look down on others.

Remember the Pharisee and the tax collector in Luke 18? They both went to the temple to pray. Verse 11 says, ***The Pharisee stood [ostentatiously] and began praying to himself [in a self-righteous way . . .].***

He wasn't praying to God; he was just trying to impress himself and the people around him. His prayer began, *'God, I thank You that I am not like the rest of men'* . . . Then he went on to list his good works: *'I fast twice a week; I pay tithes of all that I get'* (v.12).

Here comes the contrast. We hear the words of a man with a pure heart: *But the tax collector, standing at a distance, would not even raise his eyes toward heaven, but was striking his chest [in humility and repentance], saying, 'God, be merciful and gracious to me, the [especially wicked] sinner [that I am]!'* (v. 13).

The best prayer to start our day is, "Oh, God, I love You and I need You to help me today. Because if You don't help me, I can't live right before You. I want to do what's right every day, but I often end up messing up some way, God. I am so grateful for You. Thank You for loving me and meeting me right where I am. Thank You for the blood of Jesus, which cleanses me of sin. Thank You for not giving up on me. You are awesome, Father!"

MAKE A BIG DEAL OUT OF THE LITTLE THINGS

You can be as close to God as you want to be; it all depends on how much time you're willing to put into your relationship with Him. Spending time with God is so valuable. There are two ways you need to spend time with God to get closer to Him. First, you need to have time alone with God each day. I recommend the early morning hour because how you get your day started usually determines how the rest of it goes. But if morning doesn't work for you, choose the time of day that is best for you.

And second, form a habit of stopping at various times throughout the day just to say, "God, You're here." Learn to be conscious of His presence and aware of the things He does for you.

First John 4:16 says, **We have come to know [by personal observation and experience], and have believed [with deep, consistent faith] the love which God has for us....** I love how this verse says we can know the love of God **by personal observation and experience.** If we're spending time with Him regularly, we will be more sensitive to His presence and see how He is working in our lives.

Learn to be aware of His presence and aware of His love, including little things. Make a big deal out of little things.

This is one time when we need to make a big deal out of little things. Most of the time I encourage people not to be petty, to pick your battles, and don't make a big deal out of little stuff. But with God, make a big deal out of every little thing you catch Him doing for you.

His blessings can be seen in the small, everyday activities of our lives, such as an unexpected sale at the grocery store, a convenient parking spot when it's raining, or any number of things.

Be thankful for every little thing.

One way I'm practicing being more thankful each day is by taking an inventory of my day before I go to sleep that night. I think through everything I did that day and note all the little things that God did for me from the time I got up to bedtime.

If we ask Him to show us, God can open our eyes to times He has protected us and we didn't even realize it. And I'm sure there are many times God saves us from calamities that could have happened, and we weren't aware of it.

Here's a good example of this. A friend of mine was in a boat one day. Her husband was fishing, and she was riding around in the boat. She was sitting in a lawn chair and had just finished reading Psalm 91 when the boat hit a wave, knocked her chair over, and she hit her head. Right away she said, "I don't understand this. I was just reading Psalm 91 and confessing how You give Your angels charge over me. Why did I fall and hit my head?" God spoke to her heart and said, "You're not dead, are you?" I thought that was pretty cool! A better perspective of the situation was that although she hit her head, the outcome wasn't as bad as it could have been if God wasn't with her.

God is awesome, and He is so, so good to us! We just need to be mindful to notice how He is with us, blessing us, and helping us. Jesus tells us in Matthew 28:20: *. . . **"Lo, I am with you always [remaining with you perpetually—regardless of circumstance, and on every occasion], even to the end of the age."*** He's always there. And He wants you to talk about everything that concerns you.

I remember when I just couldn't believe that God wanted to be involved in everything in my life. I thought, *God's too busy; He doesn't have time to help me with some of this stuff.* Then one day when I was fixing my hair, I was getting really frustrated because it wasn't turning out the way I wanted it to. Eventually, I felt like the Holy Spirit was saying, "Pray about it." Pray about my hair?

It may seem silly to pray about your hairstyle, but the truth is, God wants to be intimately involved in your life, and He cares about you more than you know! If He's counted the hairs on your head and all your tears are in a bottle (see Matthew 10:30; Psalm 56:8), there's nothing that concerns you, beloved, that God is not concerned about.

Psalm 138:8 says, **The Lord will perfect that which concerns me . . .** (NKJV).

My experience that day was humbling because it helped me realize just how much I desperately need God to help me in everything I do, no matter how big or small it may be. This truth is hard for those of us who are so independent and take pride in having it "all together." But we can live in God's peace and joy if we will learn how to submit to Him in every situation, giving Him complete control of our lives.

I really want you to get this: You can enjoy God! You can have so much fun with Him. You were created to enjoy Him!

God loves you so much and He wants to be involved in every area of your life. The truth is, He wants to be the love of your life.